Dare to Dream

Coretta Scott King and the Civil Rights Movement

by ANGELA SHELF MEDEARIS

illustrated by Anna Rich

PUFFIN BOOKS

to Rosemary Brosnan

PUFFIN BOOKS
Published by the Penguin Group
Penguin Putnam Books for Young Readers,
345 Hudson Street, New York, New York 10014, U.S.A.
Penguin Books Ltd, 27 Wrights Lane, London W8 5TZ, England
Penguin Books Australia Ltd, Ringwood, Victoria, Australia
Penguin Books Canada Ltd, 10 Alcorn Avenue, Toronto, Ontario, Canada M4V 3B2
Penguin Books (N.Z.) Ltd, 182-190 Wairau Road, Auckland 10, New Zealand

Penguin Books Ltd, Registered Offices: Harmondsworth, Middlesex, England

First published in the United States of America by Lodestar Books,
an affiliate of Dutton Children's Books, a division of Penguin Books USA Inc., 1994
Published by Puffin Books,
a member of Penguin Putnam Books for Young Readers, 1999

10 9 8 7 6 5 4

THE LIBRARY OF CONGRESS HAS CATALOGED THE LODESTAR EDITION AS FOLLOWS:
Medearis, Angela Shelf
Dare to dream: Coretta Scott King and the civil rights movement / Angela Shelf
Medearis; illustrated by Anna Rich—1st ed.
    p.   cm.—(A Rainbow biography)
Includes bibliographical references and index.
ISBN 0-525-67426-8
1. King, Coretta Scott. 1927– —Juvenile literature. 2. King, Martin Luther, Jr.,
1929–1968—Juvenile literature. 3. Afro-Americans—Civil rights—Juvenile literature.
4. Civil rights movements—United States—History—20th century—Juvenile
literature. 5. Afro-Americans—Biography—Juvenile literature. 6. Civil rights
workers—United States—Biography—Juvenile literature. [1. King, Coretta Scott,
1927– . 2. Civil rights workers. 3. Civil rights movements—History. 4. Afro-
Americans—Biography. 5. Women—Biography.] I. Rich, Anna, ill. II. Title.
III. Series.
E185.97.K47M43 1994 323'.092—dc20 [B] 93-33573 CIP AC

Puffin Books ISBN 0-14-130202-X

Printed in the United States of America

Contents

1

Singing for Freedom

On December 5, 1956, Coretta Scott King eagerly waited backstage at the Manhattan Center in New York City. Coretta, Duke Ellington, the famous composer and conductor, and singer Harry Belafonte were presenting a special program to raise money in order to put an end to segregation in the South. Coretta's husband, Dr. Martin Luther King, Jr., was determined to win freedom and equality for African-Americans through peaceful protests. Coretta wanted to use her talent as a singer to help him.

The Center was crowded with people awaiting her appearance. Coretta had dreamed about this moment since she was a little girl. Here was her chance to sing before a huge audience! Coretta stepped out onto the stage, spoke briefly to the crowd, and sang several classical pieces in her beautiful soprano voice. Then she sang an old hymn that had a special meaning for her and the others who were working so hard to obtain justice for all races in the South:

Walk together, children, don't you get weary,
There's a great camp meeting in the promised land.

It had been a long and exciting journey for Coretta Scott King. She had traveled farther than she had ever imagined she would. Although the road had been rocky in spots, Coretta was determined to travel on until she fulfilled all her dreams. She finished her songs to thunderous applause. Coretta was pleased but not surprised that her performance had gone so well. She had been training for this moment all her life.

Coretta Scott King was born on April 27, 1927. Her mother, Bernice McMurry Scott, and her father, Obadiah, whom everyone called Obie, named their child Coretta in honor of Cora Scott, Obie's mother. Coretta's birth brought great happiness to the Scott household. But hard times soon followed.

In 1929, when Coretta was two-and-a-half years old, America entered the Great Depression. This was a period of hardship and sadness for nearly everyone in America. Banks closed, people lost their jobs, and many people went homeless and hungry.

The Depression lasted for many years. Although the Scotts had very little money, they were luckier than most because they owned the farm on which they lived. Their farm was part of a small, all-black community that was three miles from Heiberger, Alabama. The Scotts raised their own vegetables, so they always had food. Their cows, pigs, and chickens provided them with milk, meat, and fresh eggs. Although farming was hard work, the Scotts always managed to have plenty of fun and good food.

Coretta; her big sister, Edythe; and their younger brother, Obie Leonard, all helped their parents on the farm. The children made the chores go faster by singing as they worked in the fields. "This little light of mine," sang Coretta, "I'm going to let it shine." Edythe and Obie always joined in. Their songs could be heard throughout the farm as they hoed weeds, picked vegetables, milked the cows, fed the hogs and chickens, gathered eggs, and drew water from the well.

After finishing her chores, Coretta loved to play with her cousins and friends. She was small and slightly chubby, but she was strong. Coretta could outrun and outclimb any challenger, large or small.

Sometimes Coretta's quick temper got her into fights.

"Try to act more like a young lady," her mother would plead.

"I'll try," Coretta always promised. But she would forget her promise if another fight came up.[1]

Every evening after dinner, the Scotts settled down on the front porch. Mrs. Scott read and re-read *Rumpelstiltskin* and *The Little Match Girl* to the children. Coretta would often wind up the family Victrola and play one of the blues, jazz, gospel, or popular records the Scotts owned. Coretta loved singing and music. Everyone sang along with her until it was time to go to bed.

On Saturdays, the family would pile into their truck and go shopping in Marion, a small town that was twelve miles from Heiberger. Coretta and her family would spend the day buying cloth for new dresses or supplies for the farm. Although Coretta enjoyed visiting Marion, many things happened there that upset and angered her.

During the 1930s, black people were segregated, or kept apart, from whites. Because the Scotts were black, they were not allowed to try on clothes in a store where whites shopped, drink from the same water fountain that whites used, sit in the front of buses or theaters, eat in restaurants where white people ate, or check into hotels where whites stayed. Black and white children did not go to school together.

When Coretta went to the drugstore to buy an
ice cream cone, she could not go in the front door.
The drugstore in Marion was like many stores in
the South. The sign in its front window said
WHITES ONLY. Black people had to go around to the
side or back door, if they were waited on at all. All
the white children were served their choice of ice
cream first. No matter what flavor Coretta asked
for, the storekeeper always gave her whatever flavor he had too much of. Then he charged her the
same price he charged everyone else.

Black adults were treated very disrespectfully. Black men were called "boys" and black women were called "girls," even when they were old and gray. Mr. Scott refused to be treated this way. He demanded respect from anyone he met, black or white. In return, he gave people respect. He taught his children to stand up for themselves too. Mr. Scott worked hard hauling lumber for a white sawmill owner. He also taught himself how to be a barber. He saved his money, hoping to buy a new home someday. Because he dared to dream of a better life for his family, his own life was often in danger.

2

Dangerous Times

Mr. Scott received a lot of work hauling logs. He was the only black person in their community who owned a truck. Some white men became very jealous of Mr. Scott. They felt he was getting work that should go only to white people. They would stop at nothing to get him into trouble and often reported him to the police. They lied and said that he was a reckless driver. But Mr. Scott never gave up. He bought his own sawmill and fixed it up. He wanted to mill, haul, and sell his own lumber. A white man offered to buy the sawmill from Mr. Scott, but Mr. Scott refused to sell it. "Well, it won't ever do you no good," the white man said. A few days later the sawmill burned to the ground. Some people urged Mr. Scott to go to the police. But he knew that it would be useless for a black man to report the incident to the authorities.

Though he lived in constant danger, Mr. Scott did not become bitter. He worked hard and saved his money. In 1937, he was finally able to move his family out of their small, two-room frame house with its bare wooden floors and peeling wallpaper. It was a wonderful day when the Scotts moved into a larger house. Mr. Scott bought the biggest and best furniture he could find.

One night, Mr. Scott was late coming home from work. Coretta and her mother, brother, and sister were very worried about him. Finally, his truck rumbled into sight.

On his way home, Mr. Scott had been stopped by a crowd of angry white men. They stood in the road in front of his truck, armed with sticks and

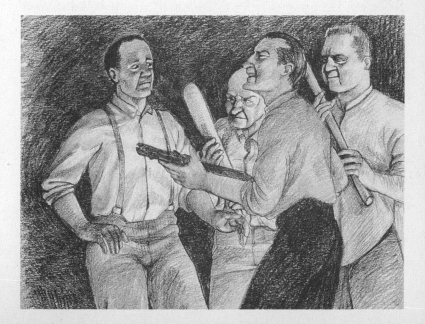

guns. "Stay in your place, Obie," they shouted at Mr. Scott. "If you don't, folks will fish you from the swamps one day."[2]

Mr. Scott stood up to them quietly and respectfully. He looked them straight in the eye.

He continued to receive threats, but he never gave in. "I may not get back," he often told Coretta's mother whenever he went deep into the woods to cut timber.[3]

Coretta grew up troubled that a courageous and proud black man like her father was constantly threatened with death in a racist society. "Why do white people treat us so badly?" Coretta asked her mother.

"You are just as good as anyone else," Coretta's mother answered. "You get an education and try to be somebody. Then you won't have to be kicked around by anybody."[4] Coretta made up her mind to get the best education possible.

3

School Days

Monday through Friday, rain or shine, Coretta, Edythe, and Obie walked three dusty miles to school. Only the white children rode school buses. Coretta watched angrily as the school bus passed them by. The Scott children were often swallowed up in a cloud of dust or splattered with mud as the bus sped away.

The white children attended school in a brick building with free textbooks, a library, and the latest equipment. Coretta and the other black children attended school in a two-room frame schoolhouse. They had to pay for their books. There was no library, and the black school had only two teachers for a hundred children in the first through the sixth grades.

Mrs. Mattie Bennett was Coretta's teacher. She

was very helpful to Coretta. Mrs. Bennett often chose Coretta to sing a solo or recite a poem whenever the school had a special program.

How excited Coretta was the day she graduated from sixth grade! She was finally going to high school. Lincoln High in Marion was the closest high school for black children. But there were no buses for the students, and Marion was too far away from the Scotts' home to travel to every day. Mr. and Mrs. Scott had been saving their money to send their children to school. The money they saved was paid to the black family in Marion that Coretta and Edythe lived with while they went to

Lincoln High. Although the girls missed their family, they were happy to be able to continue their education.

Coretta loved studying at Lincoln. Her favorite subject was music. Miss Olive J. Williams and Mrs. Frances Thomas gave Coretta her first music lessons. She studied voice, piano, and trumpet.

Because of her musical training, Coretta was chosen to be the director of the Junior Choir at her church. She created a special program for the choir that she often used as an adult. Coretta and the choir would perform such songs as "Does Jesus Care?" In between the verses of the song, Coretta would pause to explain the song's meaning. Then Coretta's sweet soprano voice would lead the choir in the next verse.

Life was going well for the Scott family until Thanksgiving night in 1942. Coretta was at school when she received a terrible phone call. The beautiful home and furniture that her parents had worked so hard to buy had burned down to the ground. The Scotts never found out how the fire started, but it looked very suspicious. The fire department refused to investigate. The Scotts had to move in with Grandfather McMurry, Mrs. Scott's father, and start all over again.

Coretta was tired of the racial hatred she faced in the South. She was tired of the names the white teenagers in Marion called her and the way they tried to push her off the sidewalk whenever she walked by. Coretta never got into a fight, but she never let anyone push her around either.

Coretta dreamed about moving up North, where blacks had a little more freedom. Edythe had graduated from Lincoln High in 1943 and had won a scholarship to Antioch College, in Yellow Springs, Ohio. She was the first black student to enroll at the small northern school.

"Oh, you'd just love it here, Coretta!" Edythe wrote to her sister from college.

Coretta wanted to go to Antioch, too, but her parents could barely afford the tuition. To help out, Coretta found a job doing housework for a white woman in Marion. The woman demanded that Coretta use the back door and say "Yes, ma'am" after almost every other word. Coretta refused to be treated so disrespectfully, and soon found herself without a job. But she was still determined to go to college somehow. It was a happy day for Coretta when she found out she'd won a four-hundred-and-fifty-dollar scholarship to Antioch! She was finally on her way up North.

Edythe made Coretta's first trip north and her first year at college a little easier. Only six black students attended Antioch. Coretta's roommates were white, but everyone got along very well. Coretta was shy at first. When anyone asked her a question, she let Edythe answer for her. But when Edythe decided to attend Ohio State in her senior year, Coretta became more outgoing.

Coretta as a student at Antioch College in Yellow Springs, Ohio, during the 1940s

Coretta majored in elementary education and music. She studied very hard. However, when she applied to the Yellow Springs School Board for a position as a student teacher, the board refused to hire her. The board members didn't want any black teachers in their district. Coretta wanted to be treated the same way that her white classmates were treated. She spoke to the president of Antioch. "Well, Corrie," he said, "what do you want us to do about it?"

"You might appeal to the school board," Coretta suggested.[5] But the president refused to help Coretta. Instead, he told her she could teach for another year at the private school on campus or in an all-black school. Coretta decided to teach another year at the private school, but she was very angry. She had come to the North from Alabama to escape segregation. Racial hatred seemed to exist everywhere, North and South.

I'll have to accept a compromise now, Coretta told herself, but I don't accept it as being right. I'm going ahead in a more determined way than ever, to do something about this situation. I don't want those who come after me to have to experience the same fate as I did.[6]

Coretta decided to join the Antioch chapter of the National Association for the Advancement of Colored People (NAACP), and the college's Race Relations Committee and Civil Liberties Committee. These groups were formed so that everyone, no matter what race, could enjoy the same rights and freedom.

While she was at Antioch, Coretta began to study music seriously. Walter F. Anderson, the head of the music department, gave her plenty of encouragement. In 1948, Dr. Anderson helped Coretta present her first public concert in Springfield, Ohio. Coretta also sang in an operetta on campus. Every time she performed, Coretta became more excited about music. She loved performing before an audience. She decided to change her major and become an opera singer.

Dr. Anderson encouraged Coretta to go to New York or Boston to study music. Even though she didn't have much money, Coretta applied to the New England Conservatory in Boston and to the Juilliard School in New York. Mrs. Jessie Treichler, another teacher, helped her apply for scholarship money.

Coretta left Antioch in 1951 before receiving her degree. She had enjoyed her college years and had learned to become much more outgoing. But Coretta still did not have enough money to attend a music conservatory to study opera. She knew that her parents would help her, but she wanted to pay for her education herself. Coretta decided to move to Boston even though she didn't have the money for her tuition at the New England Conservatory. She hoped to find a job in Boston to pay some of her expenses. Coretta was determined to make it on her own. With the money she had, she bought a train ticket to Boston.

When the train stopped in New York, Coretta called home. Her parents had a surprise for her. They told her that she had received a letter from the Noyes Foundation giving her a six-hundred-and-fifty-dollar scholarship to help pay for her musical training! Finally, she was on her way to becoming an opera singer.

4

Coretta and Martin

One day while Coretta was in her room, she received a phone call. "This is M. L. King, Jr.," the caller said. He quickly added, "A mutual friend of ours told me about you and gave me your telephone number. She said some very wonderful things about you and I'd like very much to meet you and talk to you."[7]

Coretta's friend Mary Powell had told her all about Martin Luther King, Jr., a young minister who was studying for his Ph.D. at Boston University. Coretta told Mary she wasn't interested in dating a minister. She thought Martin would be too serious.

As Martin smoothly talked on, Coretta realized he was different from most ministers she'd met. Coretta had never heard such sweet talk, but she

Coretta won a scholarship to study music at the New England Conservatory in Boston.
Courtesy of New England Conservatory

enjoyed the fun. Finally, Martin asked Coretta to meet him for lunch and she agreed.

The next day, Coretta put on her light blue suit and black coat. It was a cold, drizzly January day. She eagerly waited on the conservatory steps for Martin. When he arrived, Coretta thought, How short he seems.[8] But as Martin and Coretta talked at lunch, he seemed to grow taller. Martin Luther King, Jr., was a man who knew exactly where he was going and what he wanted to do. He impressed Coretta very much.

"Do you know something," Martin quietly said as he drove Coretta back to school after their date.

"What is that?" Coretta asked.

"You have everything I have ever wanted in a

wife. There are only four things, and you have
them all."

"I don't know how you can say that," Coretta
replied. "You don't even know me."

"Yes, I can tell," Martin said. "The four things
that I look for in a wife are character, intelligence,
personality, and beauty. And you have them all. I
want to see you again. When can I?"

"I don't know," Coretta said. "I'll have to check
my schedule. You may call me later."[9]

Coretta went up to her room hoping that Martin

wasn't serious about marriage. She was determined to have a career as an opera singer. But as the young couple continued to date, they fell deeply in love. Martin was fun to be with, and he had many of the qualities she admired in her father: a strong vision of right and wrong and a true goal in life. Coretta knew he wanted a wife who put home and family first. She couldn't decide if she should marry him or continue with her plans for a career. When she asked Edythe for advice, her sister encouraged her to marry Martin.

Coretta set aside her dreams of becoming an opera singer and began preparing herself to become a minister's wife. On June 18, 1953, Coretta and Martin were married by Martin Luther King, Sr., Martin's father, on the front lawn of her parents' newly built home in Marion, Alabama.

Martin received several job offers to teach and preach in the North. But he decided to go back home to live in the South. His father, whom everyone called Daddy King, was pastor of the Ebenezer Baptist Church in Atlanta, Georgia. Martin's family and many of his friends lived in the South, and Martin wanted to make life better for them and for other black Americans. He studied the works of many philosophers, such as John Locke, John Stuart Mill, Jean-Jacques Rousseau, Thomas Hobbes, and Aristotle. But Martin especially admired the life and work of Mahatma K. Gandhi, a man who led the people of India. Gandhi believed in using love and nonviolence to overcome evil. Martin wanted to be the kind of minister who influenced people's lives every day, not just on Sunday. "I am going to live in the South," Martin said, "because that is where I am needed."[10]

When the congregation of Dexter Avenue Baptist Church in Montgomery, Alabama, invited Martin to become their pastor, he happily accepted. Martin and Coretta returned to the South to put Martin's dreams into action.

Martin worked hard as pastor of the small church. He started several new programs so that rich and poor blacks alike felt welcome at Dexter. He visited the sick, counseled those who had special problems, performed marriage and funeral services, and spent hours working on his sermons. He joined the NAACP and the Alabama Council on Human Relations to work for a better relationship among southern blacks and whites.

Coretta made their small frame house, which the church provided, as comfortable as possible. She also worked as Martin's secretary and sang solo parts with the church choir. To Coretta's delight, she was asked to give several concerts in other cities nearby. She enjoyed performing whenever she had a chance.

On November 17, 1955, Coretta and Martin became parents. They named their baby girl Yolanda Denise, but everyone called the baby Yoki. Yoki was soon joined by her brothers, Martin, III,

and Dexter, and her baby sister Bernice, whom everyone called Bunny.

The Kings became close friends with Reverend Ralph Abernathy and his wife, Juanita, whose children were close in age to the Kings'. Coretta and Martin settled into what they thought would be a quiet life in the South. But soon after Yoki was born, a black seamstress named Rosa Parks made a decision that would change their lives forever.

5

We Shall Overcome

On December 1, 1955, Rosa Parks rode the bus home from work in downtown Montgomery. The bus was very crowded. White people boarded the bus, filling up the front. Mrs. Parks and the other black passengers paid their fare at the front door. Then they had to get off the bus and go to the back door to board. Sometimes the bus driver took the black passengers' money and then drove off before they could get through the back door. Nothing was ever done to stop this mistreatment.

The bus company refused to allow blacks and whites to enter through the same door, or sit in the same seats. Black people could not sit in the front of the bus, even if empty seats were available. They had to stand in the aisle if all the seats reserved for blacks were full. Whites had their choice of seats. If a black person was seated, a white person could order him or her to move. Many black passengers had been arrested—and several had been shot by bus drivers—for refusing to move.

Mrs. Parks was sitting with a few other black riders in the nearest seat to the "whites only" section. A white man boarded the bus, but there were no empty seats left in the front. The bus driver ordered Mrs. Parks and the other black passengers to move. Everyone stood in the aisle, except Mrs. Parks. She was sick and tired of the way the bus company treated black people. The bus driver pulled over and called the police. Mrs. Parks was handcuffed and taken to jail.

On December 2, Martin received a phone call about Mrs. Parks's arrest. Montgomery's black citizens were organizing a boycott of the buses to protest the way Mrs. Parks and other black passengers were treated.

Martin suggested that the organizers meet at Dexter Avenue Church. That evening, black people from all walks of life gathered at Dexter to organize the bus boycott. On Sunday, the city's black ministers spread the word from their pulpits. The Women's Political Council, headed by Jo Ann Robinson and Dr. Mary Fair Burks, stayed up all night running off fifty-two thousand flyers that asked everyone in the black community to stay off the buses on Monday, December 5:

Another Negro woman has been arrested and thrown into jail because she refused to get up out of her seat on the bus for a white person to sit down. . . . This must be stopped. Negroes are citizens and have rights. Until we do something to stop these arrests, they will continue. The next time, it may be you. This woman's case will come up Monday. We, therefore, are asking every Negro to stay off the buses on Monday in protest of the arrest and trial. Don't ride the buses to work, to town, to school, or anywhere on Monday. . . .[11]

Coretta received call after call about the protest. Martin drove all over town talking with black taxicab owners and black people who owned cars. He asked them to provide special fares and rides for the protesters.

Other black leaders had tried to organize protests in the past, but the protests had failed. They had never received the full cooperation of the black community. Martin worried that this protest would also fail. On the night before the boycott, Martin and Coretta sat up late into the night talking. They feared that the black community might not join together to make the bus boycott a success. There was a bus stop right near their house. They decided to get up early the next morning to see if any of the buses that stopped there were full of black passengers. If the boycott was a success, the buses would be empty.

The next morning, Coretta fixed breakfast and then settled in front of the window to wait for the bus. It was still dark outside. The bus rattled up to the stop as usual, its lights blazing. "Martin! Martin, come quickly!" Coretta shouted. "Darling, it's empty!" Coretta and Martin eagerly waited for the next bus. It, too, was empty! Black people all over town were walking, riding bicycles, taking cabs, or riding with friends. Some even used horses and buggies or rode on mules. The boycott was a success.

That evening, Martin was elected leader of the Montgomery Improvement Association, a group formed to provide guidance to the thousands of blacks participating in the bus boycott. Martin knew that by accepting the leadership of the boycott he was putting his life, and the lives of his family members, in danger. He nervously told Coretta about his decision to lead the movement. "You know that whatever you do, you have my backing," Coretta told him.[12]

Martin and the other members of the Montgomery Improvement Association tried to reason with the bus company and with city officials. But the officials refused to change their policies toward blacks. The Montgomery Improvement Association decided to continue the boycott until their demands were met. More than fifty thousand black citizens in Montgomery joined in the boycott.

On January 30, 1956, almost two months after the bus boycott started, Coretta was at home talking with a visitor, Lucy Williams. Suddenly, she heard a loud noise on the porch. "It sounds as if someone has hit the house," Coretta told her friend. "We'd better move to the back."[13]

As soon as the women left the room, a loud blast shook the house. Glass showered the living room. A bomb had split the front porch and blown a hole in the concrete floor. No one was hurt, but Coretta was shaken. This was only the first of many violent attacks against the Kings and others who fought for civil rights—freedoms guaranteed to every American under the Constitution.

After a year-long struggle, the black citizens of Montgomery won their battle against the bus company. They had walked in the cold. They had walked in the rain and in the heat of summer. They had walked together until they won their fight against injustice. "It used to be my soul was tired and my feets rested," said an elderly black woman. "Now my feet's tired, but my soul is rested."[14]

On November 13, 1956, the Supreme Court declared that segregated buses were unconstitutional. The law went into effect in Alabama on December 20, 1956. Black passengers had the right to sit anywhere on a bus. Many whites reacted violently to the Supreme Court's decision. Reverend Ralph Abernathy's home and church were among many black homes, businesses, and churches that were bombed. Twelve sticks of smoldering dynamite were left on the Kings' porch. Fortunately, the explosives didn't go off. "We must not return violence under any condition," Martin said. "I know this is difficult advice to follow, especially since we have been the victims of no less than ten bombings." White city officials finally condemned the violence and arrested those who were responsible.

Martin came under more vicious attack from people who hated what he stood for. He was threatened, arrested, and beaten. He was stabbed by an insane woman and nearly died. After every violent incident, Martin urged his followers to remain peaceful.

With Coretta's support, Martin continued to lead the nonviolent movement for racial equality. He was elected President of the Southern Christian Leadership Conference (SCLC), which was organized to spread the civil rights protest throughout the South.

Soon, Martin was so busy that he was forced to resign as pastor of Dexter Avenue Baptist Church. He became copastor under his father at Ebenezer Baptist Church in Atlanta, Georgia. Martin, Coretta, and their children moved to Atlanta, the headquarters of the SCLC.

More people eagerly joined the civil rights movement, including hundreds of young college students. Many of them decided to participate after reading Martin's book *Stride Toward Freedom,* the dramatic story of the Montgomery bus boycott.

Martin and other members of the SCLC helped

Coretta and Martin celebrating the success of the Montgomery, Alabama, bus boycott
UPI/Bettmann

organize the students into the Student Nonviolent Coordinating Committee (SNCC). Martin urged the students to use nonviolent methods in the fight for civil rights. A training program was started to teach the students how to protest peacefully. After each meeting, the students sang hymns but began changing the words to fit the civil rights movement. "We Shall Overcome" became one of the most popular songs of the movement. It was a song of hope and a source of inspiration to the thousands of civil rights workers who were beaten, jailed, and murdered for the cause of equality.

The students used many peaceful methods to fight for civil rights, such as wade-ins at segregated pools, pray-ins on courthouse steps, protest marches, and boycotts of segregated stores. They also organized voter registration drives so that black people could elect men and women who would represent them fairly.

Because of their work for civil rights, Martin and Coretta became very well known around the world. They traveled to Africa to witness the new nation of Ghana celebrate its freedom from Great Britain. They also went to India to study Gandhi's nonviolent methods. They often appeared in newspapers and magazines, and on television. Martin spent weeks away from home traveling from city to city, giving speeches about nonviolence and the civil rights movement.

Coretta also traveled around the country giving freedom concerts to raise money for the movement. Martin doubted that her concerts would raise much money. But Coretta was determined. Indeed, the concerts were a huge success, contributing more than fifty thousand dollars to the SCLC. The money that Coretta raised often came at a time when the SCLC bank account was almost empty. Martin admitted he was wrong and supported his wife's efforts. Coretta excitedly used her talent to further the cause of equality.

Now that the attention of the world was focused on the Kings, Coretta had to learn many things quickly. Since her marriage to Martin, she had been through wonderful times and dangerous times, times of celebration and times of despair. Through it all, Coretta had learned to control her quick temper and maintain serenity. Her naturally bubbly personality had become more quiet and reserved. She had learned the hard way that everything she said was not always taken the way she had meant it. She learned to choose her words and her friends wisely and carefully. But Coretta always spoke out for the causes that she believed in. "I don't make decisions lightly," Coretta said. "I weigh the impact of my actions. I've been accused of being indecisive. But I try to balance what's in my heart with my intellect."[15]

In 1962, the Women's Strike for Peace invited Coretta to travel to Geneva, Switzerland, for a meeting about the atomic test ban. This group of women from around the world believed in working together for a better future for their children and families. The conference convinced Coretta that women of all races, united in a common goal, were a powerful force for world peace.

6

Walk Together, Children

A year after Coretta traveled to Switzerland, Martin decided to join Reverend Fred Shuttlesworth in the fight for equality in Birmingham, Alabama. At that time, Birmingham was known as the "most segregated city in the South." The governor of Alabama, George Wallace, had a slogan: "Segregation Forever." He believed that white people were better than black people and that the two races should live separately. Many black people in Alabama lived under conditions similar to slavery.

For the first time, schoolchildren marched during the protests. The Children's Crusade began in Birmingham on May 2, 1963. On the second day of the march, the commissioner of public safety,

Eugene "Bull" Conner, attacked the young marchers with vicious dogs, tear gas, and high-pressure fire hoses that could peel the bark off of a tree. Hundreds of schoolchildren were bitten by police dogs and knocked down by the water from the fire hoses as they sang and marched. Nine hundred and fifty-nine children, ages six to sixteen, were arrested.

Newspaper, magazine, and television stories about the Children's Crusade shocked people around the world. President John F. Kennedy received thousands of telegrams and said he was sickened by what had occurred. More Americans began to condemn segregation and the unjust treatment of blacks. Coretta suggested that Martin call for a March on Washington. "I believe a hundred thousand people would come to the nation's capital at your invitation."[16] As a result, Martin, Coretta, and the leaders of other civil rights organizations decided that the time was right to join together for a huge "March on Washington for Jobs and Freedom."

Two hundred and fifty thousand people of all races and religions gathered together at the mall to protest the treatment of American blacks. With Coretta seated behind him, Martin spoke to the crowd. He told the people about his dream of a nation where his four children would be judged by the content of their character, not the color of their skin.

Martin and Coretta were pleased that the movement was gaining support. In 1963, President Kennedy proposed a bill that would grant equal rights to all races. But sometimes, it seemed, every gain in the fight for civil rights carried a great price. Those who opposed civil rights for blacks reacted angrily and violently to change. Many of those who worked for the cause paid with their lives.

Medgar Evers, head of the Mississippi chapter of the NAACP, was assassinated in front of his home in Jackson on June 12, 1963. On Sunday, September 15, a bomb exploded at the Sixteenth Street Baptist Church in Birmingham as four black girls put on their choir robes. The back of the church was gutted. Addie Mae Collins, Denise McNair, Carol Robertson, and Cynthia Wesley were killed in the blast. Then on November 22, President Kennedy was killed by a sniper in Dallas, Texas.

Coretta and Martin were deeply shaken by the violence. "This is what is going to happen to me also," Martin sadly told Coretta when he learned of the president's death. "I keep telling you, this is a sick society."[17] Coretta was silent. In her heart, she knew her husband was right.

President Kennedy didn't live long enough to see the impact of his civil rights bill on the treatment of blacks in America. But the new president, Lyndon Baines Johnson, worked hard to put

Kennedy's plans into action. The Civil Rights Act passed in both houses of Congress in 1964.

That was a year filled with sadness and violence. But it was also the year that Martin Luther King, Jr., received the highest award in the world bestowed upon those who work for peace. At thirty-five, Martin became one of the youngest men ever to win the Nobel Peace Prize.

Coretta and Martin, their family, and friends all flew to Oslo, Norway, where Martin received the prize at a ceremony attended by the king of Norway. It was a peaceful ending to a year filled with violence.

7

Bloody Sunday

In 1965, Martin and the other members of the SCLC decided to move deeper into Alabama to register black voters and work for civil rights. They chose Marion, Alabama, Coretta's hometown, as one of the starting points. Coretta's parents, Obie and Bernice, became active in the movement. They attended SCLC meetings and donated money to help the cause.

Although everyone worked hard, the Alabama civil rights movement was not going well. Sometimes blacks who wanted to register to vote would stand in line all day, waiting for the voter registration office to open, only to be told by the clerk that the office would remain closed for the day. At other times only one or two blacks out of a hundred would be allowed to register. Then the office would close. This went on day after day. Thirty-eight hundred protesters had been arrested in Alabama, and only thirty blacks had been allowed to register to vote. During one protest march, a young man named Jimmy Lee Jackson was shot when he tried to protect his mother and grandfather.

On March 5, 1965, Martin met with President Johnson to urge him to pass the Voting Rights Bill. This bill would guarantee Americans the right to vote regardless of race. Then he began organizing a protest march, in memory of Jimmy Lee Jackson, from Selma, Alabama, to the state capital in Montgomery fifty miles away. Governor Wallace issued an order forbidding the march. Even though he was in Washington, D.C., Martin decided that the march should continue without him. Hosea Williams and John Lewis, two SNCC leaders, led the march in his absence.

That Sunday, March 7, 1965, resulted in one of the most brutal attacks on nonviolent protesters in history. As the marchers crossed the Edmund Pettus Bridge in Selma, state troopers gave them three minutes to halt and turn around. Some of the protesters knelt to pray. After about sixty seconds, the state troopers, mounted on horses and wearing gas masks, charged into the marchers. Swinging bullwhips and billy clubs, firing canisters of tear gas and using electric cattle prods, the troopers mercilessly beat and trampled the defenseless marchers.

Running, screaming, and gagging on tear gas, some of the injured marchers fled back to Brown Chapel, the church where the march had started. The troopers chased them, trampling many of them with their horses. Some troopers even rode their horses through the church. Seventy people were taken to the hospital, and fifty more were treated for cuts, bruises, and other injuries.

As the horrified nation watched the beatings on the news that evening, the movement reached a turning point. From around the country, people gave the civil rights workers sympathy and support. Hundreds of volunteers began coming to Alabama to protest for civil rights.

Coretta had just finished a freedom concert when she heard about the violence in Alabama. She waited anxiously for a phone call from Martin. She'd heard rumors that he would be killed if he tried to lead another march across the Edmund Pettus Bridge.

When he called with the news of his plans to march on Tuesday, March 9, Coretta encouraged him. Although she was worried, she resisted her fears. She knew that the work he was doing was right. He couldn't stop now—too many people were depending on him.

Another violent event prodded President

Johnson into action. James Reeb, a white Unitarian minister from Boston, was killed by four members of the Ku Klux Klan, a powerful hate group, because he wanted to help black Alabamans.

Protests erupted around the United States. Four thousand black and white religious leaders picketed the White House demanding that the Voting Rights Bill be passed.

On March 15, President Johnson addressed Congress. "What happened in Selma," he said "is part of a far larger movement which reaches into every section and state of America. It is the effort of American Negroes to secure for themselves the full blessing of American life. Our mission is at once the oldest and the most basic of this country—to right wrong, to do justice, to serve man. Their cause must be our cause, too. Because it is not just Negroes, but really all of us, who must overcome the crippling legacy of bigotry and injustice. And we shall overcome!"[18]

"Thank goodness," Coretta said after the president's speech. "They've finally got the message my husband has been saying for years."[19]

President Johnson ordered the Alabama National Guard, as well as four thousand army troops, to protect the Selma-to-Montgomery protest marchers. Martin, Coretta, and thousands of others from around the United States marched across the Edmund Pettus Bridge. Coretta looked at Rosa

Thousands of people, black and white, joined Coretta and Martin (front and center) on their civil rights march from Selma to Montgomery, Alabama, in 1965.
UPI/Bettmann

Parks, who was marching with them, and thought about how far the civil rights movement had come. For ten long years, the struggle for civil rights had been rooted in the South. Now it was time to spread the movement into the North.

Shortly afterward, Martin began organizing a

Poor People's Campaign. Poor people of all races from across America marched on Washington and voiced their complaints. The SCLC also staged protests in Chicago, Illinois.

While in Chicago, Martin, Coretta, and their children lived in a slum apartment in one of the poorest neighborhoods. The Kings wanted to share the daily struggles of the people they were trying to help. Their apartment was up three flights of rickety stairs. There was no lock on the front door and the lobby had a dirt floor. The barely heated building smelled horrible. Coretta was shocked by these wretched conditions.

Martin, Coretta, and the SCLC staff cleaned the stairs and hallways and took out piles of garbage.

Coretta and Martin moved to a Chicago slum in 1966 to help fight the war on poverty.
AP/Wide World Photos

They met with the tenants and advised them to use their rent money to fix their apartments. They held meetings with gang members and showed them how to settle their problems nonviolently. The entire family, along with hundreds of others, marched to protest the housing conditions in Chicago.

The day after the protest march, a small incident over turning off a water hydrant exploded into a riot. The police arrested many young people and mercilessly beat others. Coretta had been scheduled to give a unity speech at the YWCA the following day. Because of the violent turn of events, she decided that something more needed to be done. Instead of giving speeches, Coretta asked the audience to support her husband's proposals, send a telegram of protest to the mayor of Chicago, and work together to make the city a better place for all races. The women in the audience made suggestions and offered their opinions. That very afternoon, Coretta and the other women in the group started an organization called Women Mobilized for Change. The membership grew to more than a thousand women. Together they worked to make life better for all races.

Operation Breadbasket, a plan for better jobs and housing, was also organized by the SCLC in Chicago. Reverend Jesse Jackson led the organization. He and his followers picketed businesses that refused to hire blacks. Coretta attended one of Reverend Jackson's meetings and was very impressed. She enjoyed the spirited gathering and the feeling of unity. Under Jackson's guidance, housing and employment conditions gradually improved for blacks in Chicago.

As America became more involved in the Vietnam War, Coretta and Martin began to work even harder for world peace. They both felt that Americans could not be free unless they were at peace.

"For a long time," Martin said, "I encouraged my wife to be active in the peace movement. Finally I could no longer stand silently by. I have spoken my convictions that this is the most evil and unjust war in the history of our country."[20]

Many of the Kings' friends disagreed with their feelings about the Vietnam War. They felt that Martin's statements against the war could hurt the civil rights movement. Martin told Coretta, "I know I'm right. I know this is an unjust and evil war. I have made my decision to oppose it, and whatever people say, I am going to stick to my convictions."[21] Coretta strongly supported her husband's decision. "You cannot believe in peace at home and not believe in international peace," she said firmly.[22]

Racial problems were occurring more and more frequently in 1967. Some blacks complained that Martin's nonviolent protests were too slow in getting results. They felt that civil rights would be achieved only by violent methods. Instead of "Peace," these protesters shouted "Black Power" and "Burn, Baby, Burn."

During the long, hot summer of 1967, riots and looting spread to cities across the United States. Martin and Coretta continued to believe that nonviolence was the only way to solve America's racial problems. Although they were sharply criticized, they continued to pursue their nonviolent work.

In Memphis, Tennessee, the Sanitation Workers' Union was nonviolently protesting poor wages and working conditions. Most of the union's members were black. During the protest march, several union members were beaten with billy clubs by the police. The union leaders called Martin and the SCLC for help. They wanted him to lead the protest scheduled for March 28, 1968. Martin agreed to lead the march. They had traveled only a few blocks when some of the younger protesters began to throw rocks and break windows. The police and National Guard moved in and beat the protesters.

Martin was unharmed, but he was extremely depressed about the violent end to the march. His supporters encouraged him to try again. He scheduled another march for April 8. On April 3, the union members held an evening rally. Martin had received several death threats that day, and he was in a solemn mood. He told the crowd that he didn't know what would happen to him in the future, but that it didn't matter. Martin spoke of reaching a mountaintop in his life. He told the audience that he was happy, not worried or fearful. Then Martin quoted a verse from *The Battle Hymn of the Republic*. "Mine eyes have seen the glory of the coming of the Lord," Martin shouted. The audience roared their approval, and Martin was overcome with emotion.

The next evening, April 4, as Martin stood on the balcony of the Lorraine Motel in Memphis, he was shot. Coretta was at home with their children when she received the terrible news. She raced to the airport so she could join her husband, but when she arrived, she learned that Martin had died. Although overcome with grief, Coretta prepared herself to tell her children that their father was never coming home again.

James Earl Ray was arrested, convicted, and sentenced to life in prison for Martin's murder. The dreamer was gone, but Coretta promised herself that the dream would live on.

8

Keeping the Dream Alive

People around the world reacted strongly to Martin's death. Some expressed an outpouring of love and concern for Coretta and her four children. Others reacted with violence. Riots exploded in more than one hundred cities across America. Meanwhile, Coretta received thousands of telegrams, letters, and phone calls. She was overwhelmed by the visitors who came to Atlanta. The small frame house that she and the children had shared with Martin overflowed with people day and night. Through it all, Coretta remained sad but calm. She greeted as many guests as she could, prepared for the funeral, and comforted her children.

The day before the funeral, Coretta, Yoki, Martin, III, and Dexter took Martin's place at the head of the Sanitation Workers' March in Memphis, Tennessee. "I think Martin would have wanted me to go," she said.[23] It was the first of many marches that Coretta would lead in his place.

After Martin's funeral service on April 9, more than one hundred fifty thousand people marched to South View Cemetery in Atlanta, Georgia. A simple mule-drawn wagon, containing Martin's casket and remains, led them through the streets lined with silent mourners.

In the years following her husband's death, Coretta committed herself to raising her children,

Coretta and her children appearing at the New England Conservatory after Martin's death
Courtesy of New England Conservatory

as well as to fulfilling Martin's dreams and a few of her own. She took his place at the head of protest marches, made hundreds of speeches, and completed many other obligations that Martin had planned before his death. She helped produce several award-winning films about their life and work. She also wrote a book titled *My Life with Martin Luther King, Jr.,* which was widely read.

In 1968, Coretta began planning a memorial to Martin's work. For years, she traveled around the country to raise the $10 million needed to build the Martin Luther King, Jr., Center for Nonviolent

The Martin Luther King, Jr., Center for Nonviolent Change in Atlanta, Georgia, attracts more than 500,000 visitors every year.
Schomburg Center for Research in Black Culture, The New York Public Library

Social Change. She reminded her audience about the ideas that Martin stood for, and vowed to continue his work. She spoke about her husband with great warmth and affection, as if he were still alive.

After many years of speeches, fund-raising, and building, the Center opened in 1981 in Atlanta, Georgia. The beautiful complex contains Martin's tomb, the Chapel of All Faiths, the King Library and Archives, a museum, office space, a gift shop, a theater, and an auditorium. More than half a million visitors tour the Center every year. People from all walks of life, from gang members to police officers, have attended classes at the Center to learn Martin's methods of solving problems nonviolently.

Coretta is the president and chief executive officer of the King Center, but her children also assist and support her work. Her older daughter, Yoki, is the Center's artistic director. She helped to write, direct, and act in *Stepping into Tomorrow*, a play about racial harmony that was presented in the Center's theater. Martin, III, is involved in politics and often attends protest marches and rallies with Coretta. Dexter is a businessman in Atlanta and has served as the Center's director of special events. Bernice, a lawyer and a minister, coordinates many of the Center's workshops for young people. Coretta is proud of the new generation of leaders who received their training at the King Center. "I have a dream too," says Coretta. "I'd like to see a more humane society, a sharing society. I dream that we will resolve our conflicts without going to war with each other."[24]

In 1986, Coretta achieved another goal she had set for herself after her husband's death: Martin's birthday, January 15, became a national holiday, a day of celebration around the United States in honor of Martin's work for peace and racial harmony.

Even though her duties at the Center keep her busy from early morning until late into the night, Coretta still finds time to do the things she enjoys. She loves making family dinners, singing, listening to music, and going to movies, concerts, the opera, plays, and baseball games. Coretta makes phone calls to friends and reads books, magazines, and newspaper articles into the wee hours of the morning. Recently, Coretta revised her autobiography, *My Life with Martin Luther King, Jr.*, and is planning a new book about her work in the civil rights movement.

Coretta also continues to be active in the international peace movement. She was arrested in front of the South African Embassy in Washington, D.C., along with Bernice and Martin, III. They were protesting the South African government's policy of racial segregation, known as apartheid. Coretta spent ten days in South Africa for the installation of Desmond Tutu as Anglican archbishop of Cape Town. He was an ardent fighter for civil rights for

Coretta and two of her children—Bernice and Martin, III—were arrested in 1985 for protesting against the South African system of apartheid.

South African blacks. While there, Coretta met with leaders of the South African movement for racial equality.

Coretta never hesitates to call high officials, from presidents to senators and representatives, to speak out on behalf of peace and justice. She has written hundreds of letters and newspaper articles to promote the cause of equality and social justice. "We have to dare to dream of genuine brotherhood and sisterhood between the races before we can bring it into being," she says.[25]

Coretta's activism continues to inspire many people.
Schomburg Center for Research in Black Culture, The New York Public Library

Coretta has weathered crisis after crisis since Martin's death. Several books and articles raised questions about his faithfulness to Coretta. Although deeply hurt, Coretta remained silent. "In the case where my husband is being attacked—he doesn't need any defense," Coretta says. "His life and his work speak for themselves."[26]

Coretta has devoted her life to keeping Martin's dreams alive. She has also worked to fulfill her own vision of a peaceful future for all races. "I never thought I could save the world," says Coretta, looking back over the years of struggle, "but I felt that I could work and make some contribution, to make things better for people who come after me."[27]

Endnotes

1. Lillie Paterson. *Coretta Scott King* (Champaign, Ill.: Garrard Publishing Company, 1977), p. 15.

2. Paterson, *Coretta Scott King*, p. 19.

3. Coretta Scott King. *My Life with Martin Luther King, Jr.*, rev. ed. (New York: Henry Holt and Company, 1993), p. 25.

4. King, *My Life with Martin Luther King, Jr.*, p. 32.

5. King, *My Life with Martin Luther King, Jr.*, p. 41.

6. King, *My Life with Martin Luther King, Jr.*, p. 41.

7. King, *My Life with Martin Luther King, Jr.*, pp. 51–52.

8. King, *My Life with Martin Luther King, Jr.*, p. 52.

9. King, *My Life with Martin Luther King, Jr.*, p. 53.

10. King, *My Life with Martin Luther King, Jr.*, p. 90.

11. William Roger Witherspoon. *Martin Luther King, Jr.: To the Mountaintop* (Garden City, N.Y.: Doubleday & Co., 1985), p. 25.

12. King, *My Life with Martin Luther King, Jr.*, p. 107.

13. King, *My Life with Martin Luther King, Jr.*, p. 117.

14. King, *My Life with Martin Luther King, Jr.*, p. 111.

15. Marian Christy, "No Stopping Coretta King," *Boston Globe* (April 12, 1987), p. A4.

16. King, *My Life with Martin Luther King, Jr.*, p. 218.

17. King, *My Life with Martin Luther King, Jr.*, p. 227.

18. King, *My Life with Martin Luther King, Jr.*, p. 246.

19. King, *My Life with Martin Luther King, Jr.*, p. 246.

20. King, *My Life with Martin Luther King, Jr.*, p. 275.

21. King, *My Life with Martin Luther King, Jr.*, pp. 275–276.

22. King, *My Life with Martin Luther King, Jr.*, p. 274.

23. King, *My Life with Martin Luther King, Jr.*, p. 302.

24. Christy, "No Stopping Coretta King," *Boston Globe* (April 12, 1987), p. A4.

25. Coretta Scott King, "1990–2035: 45 Years from Today," *Ebony* (November 1990), p. 60.

26. Lynn Norment, "Coretta Scott King: The Woman Behind the King Anniversary," *Ebony* (January 1990), pp. 116–22.

27. Norment, "Coretta Scott King: The Woman Behind the King Anniversary," pp. 116–22.

Selected Bibliography

Branch, Taylor. *Parting the Waters: America in the King Years, 1954–63.* New York: Simon and Schuster, 1988.

King, Coretta Scott. *My Life with Martin Luther King, Jr.,* rev. ed. New York: Henry Holt and Company, 1993.

Witherspoon, William Roger. *Martin Luther King, Jr.: To the Mountaintop.* Garden City, N.Y.: Doubleday & Co., 1985.

Further Reading for Children

Patrick, Diane. *Coretta Scott King.* New York: Franklin Watts, 1991.

Patterson, Lillie. *Coretta Scott King.* Champaign, Ill. Garrard Publishing Company, 1977.

Taylor, Paula. *Coretta King: A Woman of Peace.* Mankato, Minn.: Creative Education, 1974.

OTHER PUFFIN BOOKS YOU MAY ENJOY

Big Star Fallin' Mama: Five Black Women in Music
Hettie Jones

Long Journey Home: Stories from Black History
Julius Lester

Mary McLeod Bethune: Voice of Black Hope
Meltzer/Marchesi

My Life with Martin Luther King, Jr.
Coretta Scott King

They Had a Dream:
The Civil Rights Struggle from Frederick Douglass to
Marcus Garvey to Martin Luther King, Jr., and Malcolm X
Jules Archer

Witnesses to Freedom:
Young People Who Fought for Civil Rights
Belinda Rochelle

Index

Page numbers in *italics* refer to photographs.